Love Whisperings

Love Whisperings

John A. Faulkner

Shoestring Book Publishing

Paperback

ISBN: 978-1617041754

Published by; Shoestring Book Publishing.

Copyright 2013
By, John A. Faulkner
Cover art by, Faith Te
Daily Painting #129 –
Rose Painting Series: Pink Rose No. 2
All rights reserved.
Printed in the
United States of America.

No part of this book may be reproduced, stored in a retrieval system, or transmitted in any form, electronic, mechanical; or by other means whatsoever, without written permission from the author. Except for the case of brief quotations within reviews and critical articles.

Layout and design by Shoestring Book Publishing

For information address;
shoestringpublishing4u@gmail.com

Dedication

I want to dedicate this book to several people, firstly: my role model in life; my son, Michael, along with the love of his life, Shauna and to my sister in law, Peggy. Without Peggy by my side during my wife's recent bout with cancer, I would never have had the strength necessary to adorn to her sister, Annie. Next, I want to dedicate this book to the true inspiration behind it; my wife, Annie. The creation of this book was set back nine months because of Annie's bout with breast cancer. She is cancer free today by the grace of God. Any morsel of goodness I have achieved in life stems from her and her alone. I truly have been blessed by this precious soul to whom I am bequeathed. I also need to add Annie's sister, Lizzi to the dedication of this book. Lizzie was beside her sister at each and every one of her chemo treatments. She is so dear to both of us. Bless you, dear one. I need also thank Alison and Allan from Shoestring Book Publishing for their time and effort in formatting this book. Without them, this never would have been incepted. Thank you, guys.

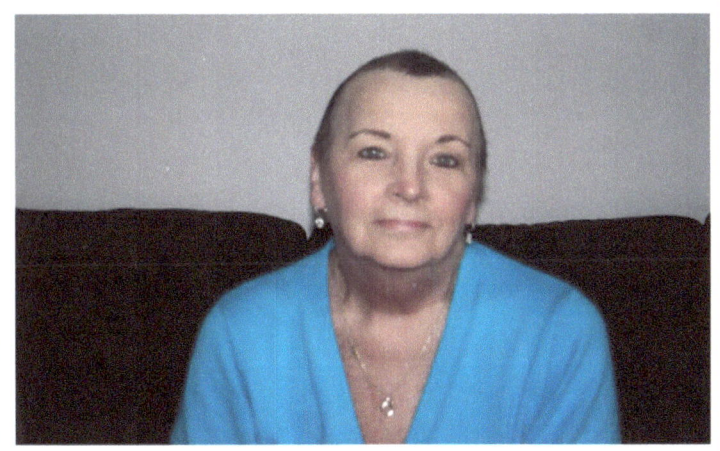

Contents

Preface	xi
Full Circle	1
Annie	2
A Woman's Pureness	3
Beholden	4
Divinity's Communion	5
Empathy's Angel	6
Breath Upon Her Mouth	7
Goodnight, English Rose	8
His Anointment	10
A Shared Vein In My Body	11
Angel's Seduction	12
Scenes	13
Whispers	14
Compassion's Embrace	16
Whispers of Despair	18
Concernment	19
A Kiss	20
A Single Ray	21
Completion	22
Absolution	23
Devoted	24
Love's Finality	25
Endearment	26
To Be Loved By You	28
Reflections	29
Deux	30
Ocean's Enslavement	31
Fate	32
Life and Death	33
Dying to Live	34
Ceaseless Kiss	35
Kitten	36

The Game of Love	38
Blessed Be	39
Love	40
Indefinable	41
His Offering of Her	42
To Be Loved By	43
Petals of Love	44
Consumation	45
Compassion's Illusion	46
Je t'aime (I Love You)	47
Us	48
Culmination	49
Indemnity	50
My Countenance	51
Intended	52
Becoming You	53
To Be A Woman	54
Tainted Fingerprints	56
Genuflection	57
To Be A Friend	58
Devotedness	59
Autumn's Seduction	60
Adorned	61
My Sweet Lady	62
Adjoined	63
Kiss	64
Making Love To You	65
You	66
Dependence	67
Cessation Denied	68
Closure	70
Final Ounce of Deceit	71
Who Knew?	72
Entireness	73
Contrasting Emotions	74

Divine Supremacy	75
Thank You Buddy	76
Due Diligence	77
Pinnacle of Devotion	78
Us	79
Unlimitless	80
Assurance	81
Still The One	82
Eternal Devotion	84
Covetousness	85
A Friend To Adore	86
Seducement	87
Devoted	88
Poetic Allegiance	89
Divinity's Thirst	90
Daddy	91
Without Definition	92
Pinnacle of Life	93
Resurrect Me	94
Fate's Decree	95
Pinnacle of Sorrow	96
Until Now	97
Love's Adornment	98
Ascension	99
Then and Now	100
Pinnacle of Equation	101
Resurrection	102
Soulmate's Invocation	103
Comforted	104
Worth the Chance	105
Couplet's Attainment	106
Conclusive Beauty	107
Subliminal Assumption	108
The End All	109
Passion's Divinity	110
Finality's Warmth	111

Resignation   112
Angel of Mine   113
Reality's Blemish   115
Author Biography   117

Preface

I have been writing poetry for many years. I joined a poetry site in 2009, and have been very active on it, both commenting on my fellow members poems, and of course posting my own. Late in 2012, I began to desire to hopefully have some of my poems published. On this site, I have posted approximately four hundred poems each year. This site has become my second home. It is precious to me, as well as all its amazing members. I adore and respect each and every one of them. I want to personally thank the two people who are responsible for this book being professionally formatted, and ready for publishing. That would be Alison and Allan, the creators of "Shoestring Book Publishing". Without them, this book would never have been incepted, Bless you all.

Full Circle

So arduous the journey has been:
timeless for you, this insidious debility,
unending torment rendered to you
without conscience or appeal,
blistering your form with relentless assault.
You were on the brink of abjuration,

yet,

through it all,
you would never abdicate to self-pity
or even a miniscule moment of despair.
I was far more than by your side, my love.
God granted me access to your essence
and by doing so, through me,
He blessed you with His miracle of faith.

Annie

Love me today,
allowing me
to absorb
the possibilities
of tomorrow.
And when
it arrives,
please soothe me
with your
delicate breath,
forevermore.
Permit me
your devotion,
one blessed day
at a time.

I love you,
my sweet Annie.
You remain
my countenance
and reason
to desire life.
Never will
this humbled man
be able to allow you
the words necessary
to express my gratitude
to the angel I love.

A Woman's Pureness

A woman is pure and selfless,
absent of envy or deceit.
She is heaven's blessing;
to be adored with reverence.

A woman is the inception of life,
the beginning of immaculacy
and the end of faithlessness,
allowing for humanity's birth.

A woman was a cherished seed,
once sacredly planted and cultivated,
bequeathing us all the spiritual growth
necessary for accession.

A woman is God's miracle to a man,
his nativity,
breath,
strength,
wisdom,
ability to love
and to be loved.;

life !

Beholden

*When this weathered man
is finally laid to rest,
no tributes or choruses of adulation
will be adorned to me.
No gold plated pagoda
with my name sake upon it
will be incepted for this amenable soul.
No!
Perhaps an austere being I have been,
yet, one who cherishes but one element in life
to be remembered for;
the only man who was ever created by God
to be granted your love.*

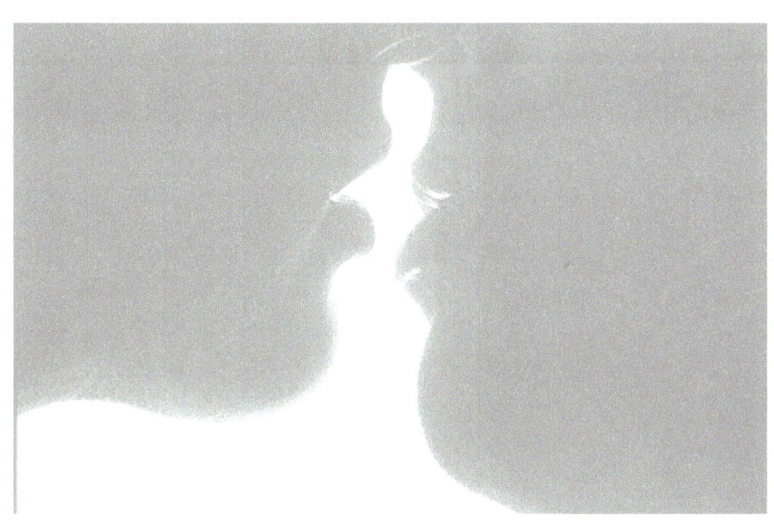

Divinity's Communion

*Whispers of love
bellow out to his burden,
transcending an inner pacification
of every infirmity he has indulged.
The pinnacle of hope is bequeathed,
a spiritual seduction has been granted,
she and he inherit oneness;*

divinity's communion.

Empathy's Angel

*The breath of her words is seductive
the aroma of them is as heaven's scent;
soft,
warm,
compassionate.*

*She writes of her benevolence to others,
soothing the anguish which encases them,
presenting them a semblance of hope,
allowing a momentary impeachment of sorrow.
No purer than she is an angel;
wings of empathy deliver her grace
to those awaiting her benediction.*

*She conceals her own affliction with humility,
never permitting its intrusion upon her
to distract from the allegiance of accountability
she holds for those blessed by her sacredness.
Bless you, sweetheart;*

be well.

Breath Upon Her Mouth

*Every breath I exhale
without bearing upon your mouth,
is one which was laid to rest
long before its time had been allotted.*

Goodnight, English Rose

You are in pain,
my love.
You cried.
I know;
because a single tear drop,
one of yours,
was gently placed
in a blessed vase,
then capped
and awarded the sanctity
of the ocean's allurement,
for destination known,
finally
and thankfully,
resting upon my bed.
As fate would allow,
that sacred tear,
yours implied,
fell upon my pillow.
I sensed it's appearance
and leaned unto it,
eager,
willing,
and able
to allow it
to become mine,
and hence;
ours.

So,
sleep, lovely one,
your tear
has become a memory
for you,
removed
by the one
who adores you;
me.
I allowed it to become mine,
and I continue
to weep away your pain
throughout this evening,
and a million more,
for the simple reason
of my adoration for you

endless.

His Anointment

*God had a plan for us
and it involved us two only.
He knew whatever I lacked
you would provide it,
and all you were without
I was able to consign to you.*

*He prevented any other man
from sensing your allure,
and more than that,
allowed it to only me.
He desired us to incept
a higher address of love
than man has ever affirmed.*

*More than all He presented us
was why He did so.
He knew we would return the favor
with humility and devotion to His name,
forever permitting Him His sacred due.
After all;*

He is God.

A Shared Vein In My Body

Embrace my hand, dear friend.
This man loves you without thought.
I am your reverent servant
to be solely used at your will.
Allow me to warm your frailties,
rendering them immune to further abscess,
for I can feel your anguish trembling
within the palate of your injured soul.

Without discretion, my precious comrade;
I am no more or less a flawed soul than you,
yet one who seeks a faulty crevice in another's spirit,
a vulnerability needing extraction,
enabling me, for the sake of my own endurance
to remove the impurity which has become ours.
You will remain as I, dear one;
blemished

yet hopeful,
beginning and End.

The end result of loving you
was the beginning of my life,
for every desolate moment lived before this
I no longer possess the memory.

Angel's Seduction

Do you have any idea,
even a possibility,
how much I love you?
Do you?
Of course you do, hon.
Why?
Simple actually:
In me, you created
the only man worthy
of your adulation
and one who will never accept
the definition of no
when you are pleading for yes
Am I right angel face?

Scenes

There are but three scenes to be played out in my life and I am blessed that you allowed me the final two, permitting me greatness:

Act 1)

The emptiness of not knowing you yet;

Act 2)

The beautification of loving you;

Act 3)

The endless possibilities yet to be encountered by us both:

"Perfection."

Whispers

From far away,
your emerald green eyes
wander to my own azurean blues,
seducing them with your clemency.

I feel your breath upon my cheeks,
warm and alluring,
as if it were mine,
like a light beam to its moon.

Don't go, dear one!
oh please, no;
I beseech you.
Permit me another effervescent moment
of intangible supplication,
granting me your indelible caress;
but one final time.

Soaring

Embrace me with a soft whisper of love
Sing to me, beautiful bird,
permit me your cleansing.

You see,
I am trembling,
fearful,
yet,
intoxicated with possibilities.
Allow me to enable them
upon your wings of hope.

Ascend, dear friend;
soar to heights yet unachieved.
Take me away, my precious attendant;
allow the gentle breeze beneath us
to dissolve my tears.
Someone
anyone
please;

love me.

Compassion's Embrace

My purse strings are depraved,
no one waits upon my needs
and I care not,
for I am but a humble servant for those in sorrow
and reaching out for compassion's embrace.

A monument does not commit my name sake,
inscribed upon a gold plaque,
awaiting my passing,
and I seek no reward in life
for living it in a manner God has instructed.
Above all,
I am not deprived of the element of frailty.
A mere human I am,
no more
or less;
flawed,
remorseful,
aching for serenity,
yet hopeful.

Although being blemished as I am,
I remain entitled to offer the emotion of love.
You, dear soul, are in pain.
I feel your sorrow upon my grieving heart,
now attached to your own.
I require your faith, my friend,
for the seed of anguish needs to be extinguished
by the prayer of two in unison of hope.
Permit me to incept you as an endearing friend,
more than equal to my humble equation.
Your pain is now mine, my sacred comrade;

we will not be denied,

I promise you.

Whispers of Despair

*The 'me' I have become to be
is the 'you' who whispered in the ears
of every woman in need of cupid's next arrow,
informing them yet another man
was removed from the stage of availability;*

yours.

Concernment

When my spirit is weakened,
moisten my cheek with a kiss.
When my will abates me,
allow me your durability.
When you stop loving me,
realize you cannot mean it;
for without you in my life
my existence will cede to finality.

A Kiss

A kiss is the conception
of our inestimable senses,
taste,
touch,
smell.

A kiss is a promise of devotion,
an exchange of benignity,
a symbol of affection,
a union of dual adherence.

A kiss is a designation of humility,
offered to another without thought,
emitted with compliance
to decorum or condolence.
A kiss is life itself;

vital.

A Single Ray

*We are all but a single ray
dwelling upon gleaming sun,
simply one of millions,
although distinctive in manner,
accordant entities
seeking to embrace
the light of hope,
and once acquired,
to illuminate our fellow man
with our brilliance.*

Completion

Me;
abandoned,
isolated.

You;
insular,
dejected.

Us;
one
now;

inimitable!

Absolution

*If you allowed me a sliver of your heart to conjoin with,
I would embellish it as an angel would her pureness
and by doing so, my own would become conclusive,
now aligned with the one dwelling in the being I love.*

Devoted

You and I are more than in love,
we are adjoined to each another
by a celestial umbilical cord,
created by He whom we serve,
allowing for an indelible linkage between us.
Within it lies the spiritual nutrition
required for a bountiful life with one another,
and for this our offering is to Him,
our defectless adherence to His Word.

Love's Finality

*If you were the last available woman in the world
and every living man courted your affection,
I would send you a poem with these humble words:*

*A million men seek out your precious heart,
yet I am the only one who desires it for your sake,
for you will never inherit the sacredness of life
until my own is affixed to yours,
and once that is incepted,
I, as well, will become whole
and in turn,
one shy of a million men will perish,
for the final sediment of love on earth
will be extinguished for ever more.*

Endearment

I was alone
on the edge of despair,
reaching out for even a granule of hope,
heart in tears,
soul in denial,
prayer dangling from quivering lips.

As an infant in dire need of its mother
I felt your presence upon my bosom,
as a warm and soothing breath
seeking out my blemished entity.
I began to plead for your embrace,
begging for cleansing.

I turned around,
an angel now present in view.
It was you, my love,
endearing my appearance
as a virgin seeking to abate her innocence
with her chosen one, now on bending knees,
permitting her the humility of his pureness.

I became engulfed in your immaculate aura,
as pure divinity lingered from my every pore
and saturated my disheartened soul,
allowing me to love once again.

*My angel,
you have redeemed me;
rescued my weakened spirit
from a state of apathy,
allowing new breath.
You have retrieved me from the pit of loneliness,
drenching me in the tranquil waters
of your amorous affection.*

*Oh, how I love thee
for seeking out my appeal for salvation.
How externally grateful I am
that you have ingested my plea,
allowing it to be the answer to your own.
Oh, how unequivocally blessed our love is
and will be for all eternity.*

I love you, sweetheart!

To Be Loved By You

*When this weathered man
is laid to final rest,
no tributes or choruses of adulation
will be bequeathed to me,
no gold plated pagoda
with my namesake upon it
will be incepted for this amenable soul.
No,
perhaps only an austere being I have been,
but one who cherishes just one element in life
to be remembered for;
the only man who was ever created
to be loved by you.*

Reflections

*Within every glance
of a mirror,
I see not only me
I see an image of two souls
dwelling upon a single face;
ours.*

Deux

Without the miracle of a resurrection,
I was born twice.
The first conception granted me life,
the second;
your own.

Ocean's Enslavement

So far away from me you are my love,
dwelling across an ocean's breadth,
alienated from my enticement and beggary for you;
flawed as an infant devoid of its mother.

Celibacy arrests my deftness to seduce your being.
I reach out for your embrace, my eternal advocate,
but your vinaceous flesh is not within attainment
and my aspiration to endure you is silenced,
allowing me a definitive betrayal of scorn's contempt.

My dear English Rose,
announce to your inner most thoughts
that they are allocated for me only
from this moment on,
for this injured heart beneath my bosom
is aching for their imminent cleansing of hopelessness.

Fate

On bended knees,
I beg you to love me.
I am a blemished man
not worthy of your affection,
yet the crevices holding my heart in place
have been tinged with the stain of sorrow
for all I crave
but cannot acquire
or be admissible to.
I may not be worthy of you

yet,

I have not a fragment of doubt
that no man alive other than I
is more worthy of your adoration.
Yes, you could love another without reservation,
but I am unable to do so,
for it is you and you alone
whom I was destined for
the first moment I laid my eyes upon you.

Life and Death

Tonight I entered slumber's enticement loving you.
Allow my one dream this evening to hear these words emit
across the sweetened breath of your lovely mouth;
I love you as well, sweetheart.
If this admission is not released to my needful heart,
then I choose to succumb, within the emptiness of the night,
rather than face another day of bereavement.

Dying to Live

If you wonder would I die for you,
my answer is a resounding no.
The reality is, my love;
I live for you.

Ceaseless Kiss

*Feeling the words emitting from your mouth
before they are even spoken,
sensing your breath upon my cheek
ahead of your actual exhale,
the scent of your kiss upon my lips
still, and forever more
even as I lay you down
upon your final resting place;
loving you always.*

Kitten

*I love you Daddy
lucky am I.
Never have I seen you
without that mint julep smile
upon your precious face,
even those moments
when I let you down.*

*You are my very own hot fudge sundae;
my ticket to slumber land each night
once your honey dew peck on my cheek
awakens the sand man's nightly obligation.
You tell me I am Daddy's head cheerleader,
the only voice he hears when the ballgame of life
heads into a direction he fears.*

*You are six feet tall;
my tailor made mountain peak.
You are my fearless angel,
the keeper of my feathers of adoration for you;
my precious craving to be even considered
your Daddy's little girl.*

Mom told me it was all right to ask you this.
Will you marry me, Daddy?
I am so afraid no other boy
could measure up to my gift of you.
Please help me, my Dad and best buddy?

"Be patient, Kitten;
I have petitioned God to allow you a man to love,
not so much of my own qualities;
more importantly your own.
You are the sum total of your Mother's blessedness
and the actuate of my now cleansed flaws.
While the man you wed will not be me,
what he will be is the one who inherited you
from the one who bequeaths you to his acquittal."

The Game of Love

They all informed me to avoid you,
that you had a one tract mind
seeking only a toy to play with;
a hobby of sorts.
They were right on, I must agree.
You did indeed use me.
You invited me to play a game,
one in which I had never learned the rules;
the game of love.

You instilled humility within me,
allowed me your compassion,
kissed me gently on the lining of my insecurities,
permitting them release.
You whispered to me that I had conquered you
in a beguiling manner unfathomable to comprehend.
If this is being labeled a game,
let's never stop playing, baby

we both win.

Blessed Be

A Mother has her child to embrace,
a tree has its branches to advocate its conformity,
a bird has its nest to shelter it from casualty,
a moon has its beams to permit acuity to it,
a flower has its bloom to enlighten it,
a kiss has two lips to convey it,
a man has his woman always above him in stature
for she is the most precious gift he endears.

Love

L onging for the ultimate value of it
O bsessed beyond words by it
V indicated for life because of it
E levated to perfection upon acquiring it.

Indefinable

There exists no single word,
and perhaps more than that,
no article of thought,
to permit me even the possibility or clarity
of relating to you how this beholden soul feels
each moment your image seduces my mind.
I could symbolize my adherence to you,
aligning it with every breath released from my mouth,
or place a delicate, erotic rose upon your apparition
embedded within my heart,
but justice would not properly accord my level of devotion,
so allow me these less than adequate words
to possibly convey my adoration for you.
More than loving you, I have become you,
and having done so,
deprived every other man alive
an opportunity for greatness.

His Offering of Her

A moment beyond my prayer for completeness,
an angel appeared before me,
asking for my hand within God's own.
As I embraced His flesh with trembling fingers,
I closed my eyes in humility's accordance.
Upon opening them, I saw before me,
an image of devotedness and empathy.
Upon the body of My Lord lay your face,
with a delicate, ambrosial smile procured upon my own.
Bless Him, my love,
He has bestowed upon us;

His own flesh.

To Be Loved By

*More sacred than being in love
is to be loved by another
without condition or restraint,
and once attained,
embraced forever
without element of thought.*

Petals of Love

Analgesic petals of love,
budding within indelible ink
inscribing upon coveting parchment
lying abandoned below,
creating poetical inception of two souls.

Consumation

You were always present within my entity;
my own cherished, endearing spirit.
Physicality of you was put on hold,
awaiting love's benediction and inception.

Seeing you that first precious moment
tinged my thoughts with passion's delirium,
rendering me incapacitated to your allure.
I was as an infant embraced by its Mother
for that miraculous first cuddle of affection.

Embracing you that indelible instant
allowed me a level of analgesia warmth
no man before me had endured;
the pureness of your feverish breath upon my own.

Making love to you for the first time
permitted this humble man of little faith
to inherit God's most precious gift in my favor,
Heaven's most absolute compliance;

you, sweetheart,

you alone.

Compassion's Illusion

I beseech a devout appeal from you;
realizing such an emotion spoken from your lips
will never be brandished from within your heart.
The deceit is mine only to ingest
and not intended for your resolve.
Sweet woman, blessed friend,
permit me but three syllables of devotion,
whispered into my essence,
one sacred moment before my final breath;

"I love you."

Je t'aime (I Love You)

You are the arteries flowing
throughout my body,
the analeptic lining of my heart,
keeper of my soul,
guardian of my subsistence,
and most cherished;
the curator of my destiny.

Us

*If I were granted the unique possibility
of experiencing that precious allure
of falling in love with you once again,
I would change but one element
of that surreal moment in time.*

*I wish I knew then what I realize now
and could have informed you at that hour.
More than being allowed to love you,
I am blessed to have become you,
and by the blueprint of our assemblage,
we have inherited the only singular plural ever created;*

"us."

Culmination

Draw nearer to me.
Closer, baby.
Allow me a single whisper
upon your feathered ear.
Every beat of my heart
now seduced by your image
is flaunting their desire
for conveyance of our impetration.
Remember this moment
for the lifetime of two.
Only once will these words
be spoken by this proud man,
and to you they breathlessly emit;

I have fallen in love with you.

Indemnity

*How you have permitted yourself
to love this austere man of nullity
is beyond my ability to discern.
When I created and petitioned
a benevolent prayer to heaven,
pleading for inner relief from seclusion,
never could I have truly realized
or even possibly conceived the notion
that the pastoral appearance of you
would inherit my subsistence;
composing a sphere of absolution.*

My Countenance

Dear cherished life;
I adore you
without condition or hesitance.
You have granted me,
as always,
another day of belief in geniality.

Bless you for seducing me
every moment of my life
with your compassion and grace.
We have become an eternal couplet
inseparable from one another;
a timeless union of sacred bouquet
composed with the fragrance of deification.

Intended

By the endowment of a higher power,
we were both sanctioned by his grace at birth,
with the pureness and blessing of oneness,
destined for adornment by one another
at the sacred moment of his will.

In my mother's cradle, upon first breath,
I adoringly saw a lovely halo upon her form,
and aside it, another,
gently glowing above the image of an embryo in waiting,
one so adoring, I was drawn to its appeal without tolerance.

The consequence of time was our only barrier,
yet never did we doubt fate's inclination.
We were both spared the invalidation of wonder.
Set in unbreakable stone was our allocation;
to be united as intended,
not pretended;

we made it, baby.

Becoming You

Far greater than loving you,
I endeavored to become you,
and when you allowed me,
your thoughts became my very own
a moment before they entered your mind.
Never again will I ache for your embrace,
for the warmth of your heart will bond us forever.
You are more than the love of my life,
you are my life,
and being so,
I worship you as I would my god.

To Be A Woman

To be a woman is a gift,
a true privilege,
an honor,
blessing.

The miracle of a woman
is simply her presence,
and the dignity she commands
for her value
to all of us.

A woman is the origin
of all our dreams and goals

our beginning...

of what life has to offer
if we truly want it,
because of her

only...

A woman is our salvation,
the seed leading to our growth,
because of her desire
for the same.

The Lord created women
for His own sake,
and for ours,
for her own conception of

morality...

for all of us...

*A woman has a degree of beauty
beyond our capacity to comprehend,
for this is the mystery
of her attainment,
and purpose*

ours...

*Women are selfless,
committed to those
other than themselves,
for this is their intent*

giving...

to all...

Tainted Fingerprints

*Fingerprints of you,
no longer the scent of freshness,
scattered within my heart,
benumbed in grief's cleave,
wilted,
basted in isolation's residue,
finally;*

*cremated in the sphere
of your delectation.*

Genuflection

Perfumed thoughts of your image
seduce the delicate pores of my amiable skin,
granting me the fragrance of covetousness.
You slay my will with your felicitous enticement,
rendering me with an intolerable quench for your devoutness.
Far more than loving you,
I am fearful of losing you,
and if I did,
my greatest poem will never have been written.

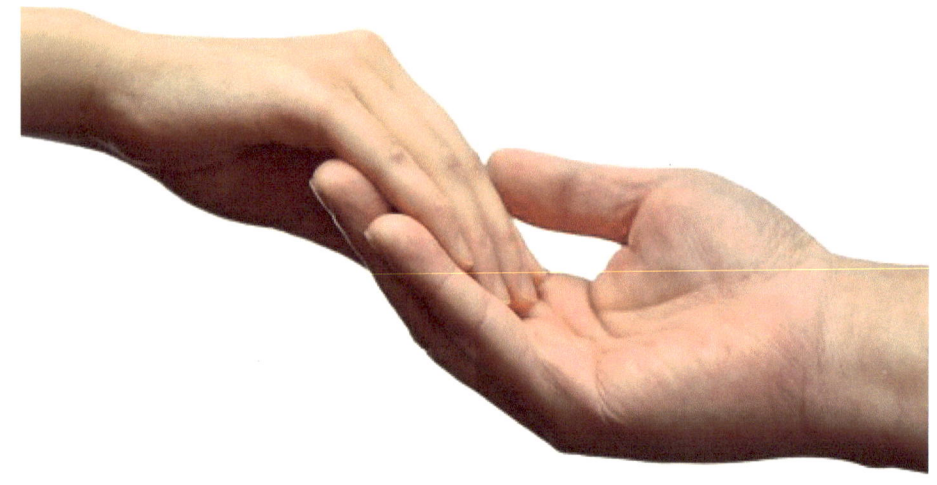

To Be A Friend

More than adoring you,
I adhere to your elegance of thought,
for you have blessed me
with more than any man could earn;
your unbridled devotion.

Devotedness

Infant's breath upon her own;
the sacredness of assemblage.
Mother's beloved tears fall gently
upon child's vulnerability,
allowing for love's immensity;
completeness is assimilated.

Supplanted gaze upon one another;
perfection's duet is assembled.
both are granted divinity's bouquet,
fetal accession now absolute;
life is adorned.

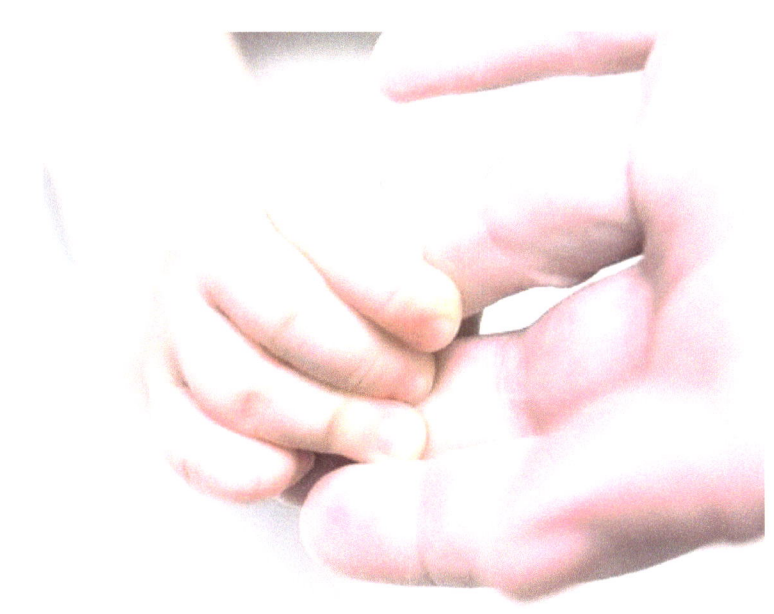

Autumn's Seduction

Serenade of autumn's hymnal;
affecting and ebullient.
Nature's arousal is enkindled,
awakened by morning's embrace.

Silhouettes of passion
plead for devotion's enticement.
Calming breezes of impenetrable allure
gently warm hearts enshrouded in solitude,
those seeking resurrection from seclusion;
pleading now for a lover's evocation.

Splendour of leaves rustling
in seductive hues of intimacy.
Harvest moon elevates arousal.
Amiability,
once again,
is inherited to another;

Gemini's seduction.

Adorned

*Benevolent
Immutable,
Endearing,
Absolute,
Flawless,
Devoted,
Selfless,
Adored;*

A woman.

*To each of you,
I allow a tear
of gratitude
and humility.
More than I
revere you,
love you I do;
without the element
of thought's conception.*

My Sweet Lady

You allow me your ampleness,
clemency,
benignity,
ethicality,
humility,
breath.

No meager soul,
such as I,
could feel as desirous for you
as this man has attained.
You are my eternal shepherd
and boundless divinity of pureness.

You more than love me, dear baroness,
I have been delivered to the sanctity
of thou cherished and alleviating bosom
by your maidenly embrace of assurance.

You are my Lady.
To most others;
their Lord.
More effectual;
bless me, my sweet God.

Adjoined

Our alignment,
so rare and precious;
an exact alteration
requiring no mending.
Is this possible?
It is, dear confidant,
it truly is.
You have become my twin,
that missing dimple on my barren cheek.

More than desiring to make love to you,
I ache for the virtue of simply embracing your form,
to seduce you with selfless adoration,
and fornicate with your empathy for me.
Any sane man, with sound mind
would be a fool not to be willing to beg
for the possession of but one of your breaths.

Kiss

Defining a kiss
is as futile as embracing
the actual definition of love;
one which,
if it were possible,
would blemish the capacity
of Webster's accreditation.

A kiss, to me,
but a humbled soul,
cannot be permitted to unleash
its actual clarification to those
incapable of acquiring such level
of thought accession.

A kiss is far greater
than the anointing of dualistic seductive lips
entangling the moistened arousal
of another's plea for exhilaration.
The allure of wonderment
emits the cherished appellation
of its true meaning;

indefinable !

Making Love To You

*Every precious moment
you allow this blessed man
the dignity and bestowal
of making love to you,
each beating heart in this world
at that precious ascendancy in time,
skips one;
in reverence to us.*

*Far greater than loving you
is the ache I embellish
every second your image
seduces my thought process.
Your alluring scent allows me
the gift of humility and strength.
Your ceaseless essence of temptation
slays my ability to function.
Bless you sweetheart;
this man craves you
as no other is permitted.*

You

*If,
after being blessed
to be consigned your love
in this,
the only life I will ever be granted;
then this contrite man can do no more
than offer a prayer of supreme gratitude
to a power far greater than I ;*

you.

Dependence

You used to be simply my lover.
Now you have become an addiction
never to be recovered from.
It frightens me to imagine a detox from you.
The healing antidote would kill me.
I crave another hit from you;

now !

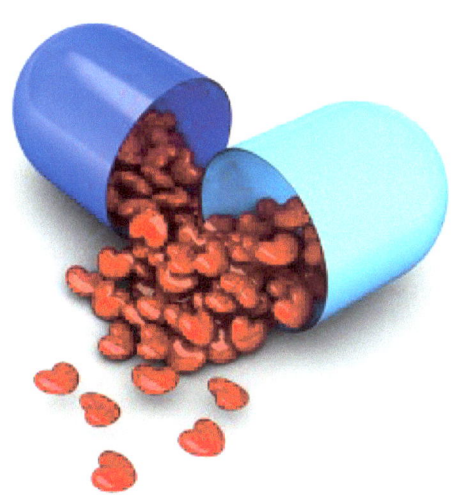

Cessation Denied

Finally;
benediction,
normalcy,
healing.
My life's partner
and lover
of my soul,
no longer governed
by diffidence.
She, by her vulnerability,
reverted to the needs of a daughter
to her then, by necessity,
make shift paternal husband;
me.

Whistling has returned,
even an off key song
bellowing from
her resurrected lips
are now ones
which have
come alive
as before.
The demon of flesh
shed insult
upon her.
It has
been slain
by the faith
of two souls
refusing it's trespasses
against us.

*We have
been accorded
continuance of
our lives together.
This monster removed
one quarter of her dermis,
singed her spirit
with the flame of doubt,
moistened her faith
with droplets
of deceit*

yet;

*it never
even considered
the faint possibility
of another entity
more supreme to it
advancing to suppress
its intention.
Behold,
you malady of blight;
you miscalculated.
God had
another option
to present;
His own!
His promise
came to pass;*

be gone, you.

Closure

I love you
each and every one of you
even those who have blemished me,
and especially those whom I have injured.
No questions asked or needed
or thought process required.
By the word and promise of God,
we are reborn to one another;
a resurrection of forgiveness

a new beginning.

Final Ounce of Deceit

Liquor scented thoughts
seduce her deformed mind,
now pulsating beyond its limit,
with no amendment to endear.

No rose garden blossoming in her life;
now only deceased buds once bloomed in hope.
She weeps without tears,
for the drought of reason is unable to formulate them.

Another shot of doubt is consumed,
yet,
unlike before,
the pain is not anesthetized.
Wonderment is exhumed;
reality is accepted;

cessation is granted.

Who Knew?

Hey!
Sorry to wake you, baby.
I needed to inform you
that every other man in the world
worthy of you, except me,
has been informed by God
to seek another.
We just became inclusive.
Wow,
this prayer thing really works;

who knew?

Entireness

I have loved you,
with endless allurement and spiritual compliance
since that ineffable eminence in time
when God,
in all His glorious compassion,
allowed this flawed man of inconsequence
and misdemeanant unworthiness,
the inheritance of His most absolute benevolence;

you.

Contrasting Emotions

Without you;

foul scented breath,
bankrupt heart,
calloused soul,
tears, so dried by sorrow
unable to be released.

With you;

ambrosial breath,
heart with perpetual beat,
divineness of soul,
tears, hydrated by love
flowing with beads of assurance.

Divine Supremacy

Only one entity I am able to appoint my savior,
and that is my God.
Having accredited that sacred gift of necessity,
this humble man of grateful platitude
credits you not as my savior,
rather saving me from wandering from His Word
You have enabled me to accept Him
and in return, He has bequeathed you to me

bless you, my love.

Thank You Buddy

I am no more or less than you;
a flawed soul seeking to right the ship of remorse.
Complaining, I no longer embellish,
for the realization of the inability of this man
to continue to accept my own will to spiritually govern my life
has been replaced by He whom has awarded me His own,
one day at a time;

baby steps.

Due Diligence

Home sweet home finally,
yet,
doubt and fear are her gruesome seducers,
while an aggrieved heart bleeds for self-piety.

So long this journey in dire isolation;
too many tears to permit the flow of even one more drop.
Alienated,
needful,
empty,
in mourning for that sacred and desired feeling she required
which was aborted before even presented to her.
Her life's consequence;
always just a step behind the angel of hope.

Seesaw emotions dominate her will for betterment;
not if,
but when
her faith in God will supplant His will upon this precious soul,
as His will be done,
in His own decree and time.
She is not standing alone in this transformation,
for this flawed man holds priceless the honor of friendship with her.
Enduring patience, my friend,
you are soon to be blessed.
Pray and believe;
the release of your sorrow is now encasing your entity.
Hold dearly your faith in Him;

He is embracing you now,

I promise.

Pinnacle of Devotion

I love you as an angel would her God;
without the element of thought.
I love you as a Mother
a moment after conceiving her first child.
I love you as a prayer
for the gift of forgiveness
answered.

I love you for what you represent to me;
my very breath.
I love you as a man should
for being blessed by you;

without condition!

Us

There is only one element I can offer you
as any other man is allowed to as well.
I love you, as they do,
but;
I require you more than them,
for you have become the breath I need for survival.
More than loving you,
I have become you.
Please;
crave me as I do you.
Inhale me, baby.
Consume all I value to you;
take my breath away, darling

allow me to seduce your will.

Unlimitless

I would obey any request
you desired me to implement
to your satisfaction and benefit.
I would present you a glimmering falling star
if you desired such a bounty.
I would imprint my love for you to see
on the face of the moon in evening's splendor.
I would offer you the passage to heaven if God allowed,
with me embracing your soul for eternity's passage;

test me, sweetheart?

Assurance

In the event you fall out of love with me,
I have asked God to create a duplicate of you
to be placed in the conservatory of heaven's portage,
for application, if needed.
You see, baby,
I could never live without you loving me.
I am simply doing all I am able
to overcome that possibility;

I crave you beyond reason.

Still The One

Six decades of loving you,
and you know what.
We have had a ball,
you and I.
We stuck together through life's bruises,
yet we never gave in to them,
and for that, we continued to gain strength.

I remember our first kiss.
like a puppy licking its first special treat.
I was thinking to myself;
I just kissed a princess.
We both knew at that moment this was to be forever.
neither one of us experienced not even a seedling of doubt.

You bequeathed me five precious daughters
and a few private thoughts of finally having a son,
but blessed we were,
although I have to admit:
you girls had a six to one advantage over me
and I loved it.
Boy; did you spoil me rotten.

Our journey is in its final phase,
yet regret never inhibits our entity.
The good Lord hit a home run
uniting us together,
as only He is allowed.
More than loving one another
we have become each other,
two souls bonded with a spiritual adhesive,
created my fate's intention.
Goodnight , sweetheart:

kisses?

Eternal Devotion

Only a moment ago
I passed away
without a single regret.
I died with you as the only thought
encasing my humbled mind at that ascendancy.
Your love of me allowed this grateful soul the gift of life.
Your belief in me allowed this man strength in death,
for in God's time, we will be reunited forever, my love.

Covetousness

No man alive could love you in the manner
as the one you are in love with,
yet I thirst for more of you
than is possible or allowed.
My entity suffers remorse and sorrow
when I am not nestled in your embrace.
I crave you as no other is accorded.

My allure for you
has anointed me a level of sensual addiction
which renders me on the cusp of unconsciousness.
I obsess about you
as no human mind can register.
More than loving you,
I beg to consume you,
and in doing so;
permitting us a level of passion
incomprehensible for a mere mortal to fathom.
Allow my palate more exposure to your desire;
grant me your endowment of covetousness;

I beg you, my love !

A Friend To Adore

You and I,
not in love,
*simply **loved***
by one another
in the form
of a sacred comrade,
to admire as a friend,
whose imprint of adoration
is embedded upon each other's heart.

Allow me to share with you
my inner most thoughts of tribulation,
as well as my blessedness for life itself.
I am not in love with you, my friend.
I am in love with the necessity
we hold for each other's acceptation.
You are not my lover,
yet you remain a crowned jewel,
appearing near the top
of my most prized valuables.

Seducement

I never meant to fall in love with you.
I simply required a faithful comrade to acquire.
You had alternative ideas of your own.
Sense did you, my hesitation
to permit my submission to your desire of me.
I fought it with every molecule in my entity.

This flawed man was not worthy of your deference.
What measure of contentment could I possibly attend to you?
You supplied me with an equivalent positive
to counteract each of my negatives,
and then it hit me.
No was not an option for you.
You willed me to love you,
didn't you baby,
and in doing so,
I was bequeathed a plateau of sanctimony few souls attain.
Seduced, I was, with my one single asset remaining;

you.

Devoted

Loving you has permitted me
what no other man could ever attain;
the only woman God has ever created
with the veil of her soul adorned to my own
and a singular, endearing heart allowing breath
for two of His most precious blessings;

us.

Poetic Allegiance

My adoring brethren;
you view my humble poems of love
as I appraise your own, in hallowed awe.
When I devour, with revered approval
each and every passage of your verse,
my own meager, cadence approaches contriteness.
Envious assertions have no appointment in our arena
for we are all the epitome of equality.
We view ourselves as the seducers of language,
adulating one another's engraved composition
with a level of adoration few are able to attain

bless you all.

Divinity's Thirst

I feel the soothing warmth of your divine breath
upon my depleted essence
at every moment in my life.
It is as if you are haunting me
into inviting you into my brothel of anguish
to allow you to accomplish
what you offer to all whom you have created;
endurance!
Why does that induce fear in me, dear Lord?
We both know;
don't we ?
Remain believing in me, Father,
our communion is approaching.
Please abate my diffidence to it?

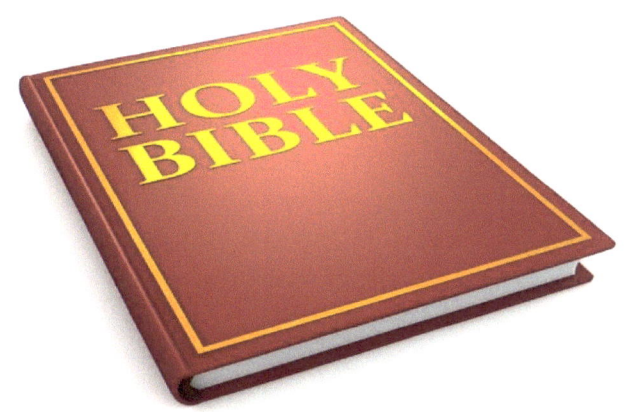

Daddy

Allow me the humility of self-awareness
for only in it can I seek relief of burden.
No end games allowed in heaven's check mate.
Winning or losing,
simplicity,
live or die.
Tell me, My Dear Creator,
am I salvageable?
Let's talk.
I need you more than ever.
Your final verse will complete my poem,
all about us, my Lord…
Your call, sir;
pray, or pray more?

Tell me please.

Without Definition

What increment of words or thoughts can fully convey
the actual breadth of love this grateful man holds for you?
This humble, mortal being has no antiphony to supplant you with.
And so I, with more than a fragment of regret,
can only offer you my eternal sustenance. My Love;
a single breath to sustain two souls in love.
Believe in the miracle of us
forever.
We will conquer.
I promise; My Love!

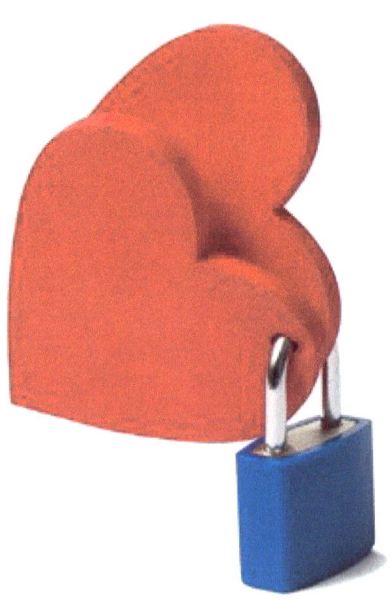

Pinnacle of Life

If my life
ceased to exist
beyond this very moment,
then
no more could this man
have attained in it
than loving you.
For a plateau beyond that
could never exist
unless
I were gifted
another one of you
to adore.

Resurrect Me

Did I ever reveal my passion for you?
I believe not, dear sweet petal of my absolution.
You are my morality and countenance.
Shame on me, for the absence of deserving thou.
You activate me,
drive me,
I believe love me.
Fool are you
though,
for accepting my blemishes.
Never cease believing in me.
I grant you my essence for your amendment.
Take my soul, I beg you.
Lead me to the sphere of your assurance;
resurrect me with your enduring pureness.

Fate's Decree

You hear me in silence.
My words do not emit to you,
yet they are incepted within your own heart
as a seductive, illusive whisper,
without the element of sound.
For we,
it appears,
have been engaged by fate's decree.

I allude to your anguish,
you comfort my own,
seduced are we by the allure of wonderment,
disallowing approval of reality's decor.
Perhaps we are no greater
than an analgesia for one another,
a supplication of endearment for two souls
seeking the innocence of empathy.

Pinnacle of Sorrow

My heart
weeping with sorrow's ink,
my soul
leaving my palate tasteless,
my love
in pain, yet without need of admittance.

Me;
supportive, balanced,
yet anguished,
seeking inner durability,
begging not for my decree,
but for her;
my countenance.

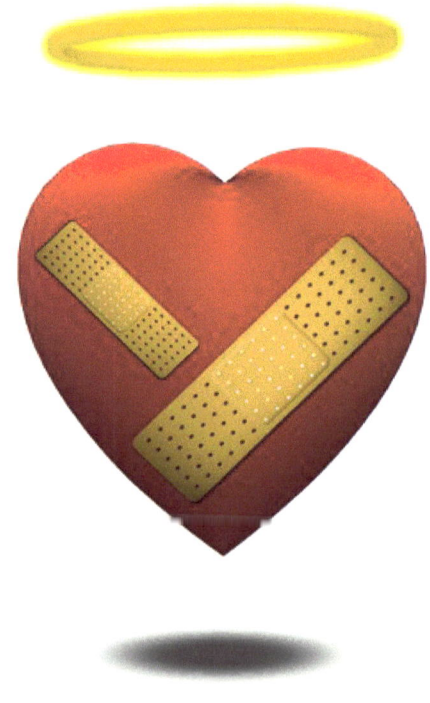

Until Now

Never before
have I known the true meaning of love as I inherit now.
Never before
have I felt the level of empathy I feel towards you
as I do at this moment of despair for me.
Never before
have I seen you this vulnerable and inwardly brittle
as I watch you refuse to give in to your affliction.

Never before
has another human being consumed my entity
in a manner as you do;
an attributive level of entireness I dearly embrace.
My heart is no longer in abeyance,
it is bathing in the enrichment of the adoration
we both place for one another.
Your unfailing strength has resurrected my own.

Sleep gently, My Love;
a smile has once again incepted upon my face.
You are my embodiment to life.
I love you now and forever.

Love's Adornment

To be truly yours
is to become you;
loving without assuage,
adoring without reflection.

To be truly yours
is to become you;
forgiving as a Mother
to her aggrieved child.

To be truly yours
is to become you;
pure, yet humble,
without need for cognizance.

To be truly yours
is to become you;
a prayer delivered
for a petition of deference.

To be truly yours
is to become you;
devoted without abeyance,
willed by faithfulness.

To be truly yours
is to become you;
the only soul in life
you have been blessed with
for eternity's slumber.

Ascension

Going it alone
abandoned ceaselessly,
singular now, though.
Wings ascended to hope,
seeking not another to love,
only herself,
once a delicate and budding flower
with cogency and allurement;
now transitioning to flee
the restraint of mediocracy.

Then and Now

Before you;
alienated,
catatonic,
affectless,
sorrowful,
depleted.

With you;
consecrated,
beautified,
devoted,
resurrected,
absolute.

Pinnacle of Equation

At the identical moment you were conceived,
I was gifted my own beginning from a mother's deification.
The two of us, aligned together, yet encased in separate embryo's,
with a sacred promise of our impending reconciliation as God intends,
will one day become as one, a union of inseparability.
We are adjoined together with the miracle of divinity,
as no other couplet is decreed.
Two souls have been granted congenital defectlessness for one another.

I felt your first tear emitted upon your cherished emergence,
as you dignified my own with your awareness of my initial weep as well.
Embodiment of love's intention was anointed and conjoined;
the infinite address of ecclesiastic delirium.
Far greater than loving you,
we have been bequeathed the essence of us;
a single entity of pureness.

Resurrection

Autumn breeze imparts my essence,
singe of allayment caresses my cheek,
inducing clemency of burden.
Tenderness of assurance is incepted,
weight of sorrow's penance laid to rest,
the derivation of grief is slain;

bring it on, life !

Soulmate's Invocation

*When one acquires a precious confidant,
that cherished soul who will, without thought,
sacrifice the implementation of self-address
for the sake of the one you love, excluding of condition;
then the face of heaven emits a tear of acceptance.*

*Bless you, Dear Advocate:
my heart belongs to another.
Yet, be assured my soul has inherited your spirit,
allowing us the uniqueness of fate's decree.
Embrace my quivering hand, my friend,
the one now empty awaiting the warmth of your cogency;
the other, the one spoken for,
seducing the one who has allowed me life.*

Bless you both.

Comforted

I am waltzing in slumber's lullaby,
comforted by dream's allure.
She is, as well,
contented
without abscess;
in peace …

home again.

Worth the Chance

If I were able to treasure you,
even an intimate sliver of indentation
beyond the emotion of love,
then I would be deceased.
For no man has enough breath
to survive this phenomenon of impossibility.
Having stated that,
I am prepared to die attempting to do so.

Couplet's Attainment

If you ever attain that same crimson level of adornment
I place upon you every moment of my appreciative life,
then allow me to qualify these few confiding thoughts.
I humbly beg you to accept me, Dear Comrade of mine,
as the flawed human being I am,
yet striving for betterment of diligence.
I become weakened at times of instability,
but fearful too often of plea for remedy,
drained by the advertency of losing you
and becoming once again extinct from righteousness.
The only singular duet which exists in this universe
is the conception of two souls melding into an article of one;
us.

I am no more than a meager vessel your blood requires to travel through,
allowing us both the attainment of its richness and hymnal sacredness.
Far greater than loving me,
you have restored my faith in myself,
permitting me your own.

Bless you.

Conclusive Beauty

I do not seek the sensuality of Cleopatra
nor the plead from a Juliette for pleasure's invite.
All I require from you, sweet woman,
are your seductive eyes making love to my own,
rendering me useless to any other woman,
domineering me into a celestial state of bliss,
undefined, satiable appetence
no other man will ever be allowed.

Do you comprehend, sweetheart?
Greater than being in love with you,
I worship you.
You are my implant of desire,
a regeneration of hope.
The only appeal I hold for you
lies not on the surface of your form,
rather within your inner allocation of loveliness.

Subliminal Assumption

*In every man's heart,
a bouquet of indulgence
dignifies his passion for her.
Observance of adornment is induced
rather than suppressed,
evolution of desire is implanted.
Youth is made love to
on a bed of angel wings
under the heat of internal achedness;
dearness of completion is assembled.
Entireness is incepted,
a miracle's embryo is birthed;
resolution for wholeness appears.
Melody in tune with devotion is sung,
invoice for love granted is issued,
never to be paid in full,
discretion is implemented;
you have become my entire essence.*

The End All

*I would forfeit the rest of my life
for but only one moment of your own,
and in doing so,
what more could I ever attain?
Perfection rarely intrudes
upon a yearning soul in need.
Allow me,
I beseech you.*

Passion's Divinity

When I made love to you, early on,
I acquired a level of triumph
only a gladiator is allowed.
As I began to fall in love with you,
with an insatiable languishment of us
and aching beyond the intellect of man's limit,
the reality of it impregnated me
with an advocated degree of spiritual lust
gifted only to the benevolence of a god.
Worshiping you was far greater than coveting;
it humbly urged a prayer blessed by a higher power,
petitioning for a sacred, insurmountable urge
for the delectation of faithfulness.

Finality's Warmth

Death is approaching
yet I fear not it's implication,
for my preparedness of finality
has endured me for this moment.

Could have
should have,
what does it matter now?
The journey is complete;
heading home without regret.

Who have I injured along the way?
Who has testified against me in silence?
Did I accomplish more or less than desired?
Choices and guessing have now been extinguished,
so I discard faithless canticles of wonderment
into the cycle bin of acceptance.

All these years
for better or worse,
indignation has been finally slain.
The ashes of my soul,
now encased in hibernation's care,
will be passed on to my only heir,
you, Lord.

Who else?

Resignation

She never bemoans her plight.
Her tears unwilling to be released
and exposed to those she loves.
Cry, my sweet angel.
I need the moisture of your eye ducts
to flush out the barrenness of my own.

So beguiled of me to allege
even a murmur of a complaint,
but I feel compelled to plead out
for the woman I adore,
who, for a reason I do not comprehend,
falls silenced to the decree of plea for mercy.

Allow this ineligible man your blessing, my Lord.
I humbly beg you.
Allow me the worthiness of your thirteenth disciple,
if only for a precious moment.
To apply your immaculate cleansing to her affliction,
in your sacred name.
Father, please,
I am trembling.
Embrace her, through me.
Absolution.

Sorrow's membrane,
despoiling out it's domain of acquittal,
enkindles a single remaining molecule of hope;
aspiration is resurrected.

Angel of Mine

*This simple yet humble man
with constricted decree of value
at this indelible moment of my life
with but one longing to acquire
before my entity is consumed by finality;
your endearment to me, dear precious one,*

what more could I ever desire?

Our Waltz

Seductive first arrhythmia,
ambrosial scent,
triple cadence allure,
effortless, unhesitant actuation,
intoxicating embrace.

Briskly adorned with aplomb,
rise and fall of chest cavity's warmth,
under arm turns of grace,
solo spins accentuated by duplicity.
Slowed down tempo,
twin sets of eyes seducing one another.
Desire's broth is inhaled.

Reality's Blemish

*Whichever woman I may
attempt to cherish
or tenderly adore,
possibly fall in love with,
will be tormented by the frigidity
of my appeal to her,
for she can never be the one
who has inherited the bounty
for the deliverance of my completion.
You baby,*

only you

Author Biography

Every positive element in my life comes from my wife, Annie, and that includes inspiration, humility, perseverance, hope, and love. In July of 2012, she was diagnosed with breast cancer. She had her surgery two months later and chemotherapy treatments were extremely invasive for her. But she got through it with her own inner strength and determination. I am blessed to have the love of my life cancer free. I put this project on hold for nine months; until Annie was fully healed. All my inspiration for my love poetry comes from her. Life is good, thank God.

www.ingramcontent.com/pod-product-compliance
Lightning Source LLC
Chambersburg PA
CBHW042304150426
43197CB00001B/5